SCULPTURE FROM JUNK

SCULPTURE *from Junk*

Henry N. Rasmusen

and Art Grant

Reinhold Publishing Corporation
A subsidiary of Chapman-Reinhold, Inc.
New York   Amsterdam   London
An Art Horizons Book

Acknowledgements

Sincere appreciation is extended to the many museums, galleries, and individuals who cooperated by answering requests for information and illustrations for this book. There are too many to list here but credit is given next to the titles of the various photographs they submitted.

The authors are grateful to the junk sculpture students of the San Francisco State College Downtown Center for their enthusiastic cooperation.

Special thanks are due to the following artist-photographers who contributed time and talents beyond the ordinary: Hal Rumel, Salt Lake City; Frank Mulvey, Baltimore; Ernest E. Burden, San Francisco; Claire Isaacs, San Bernardino; Ralph Gibson, Los Angeles; and Glenn E. Mitchell, Ray Anderson, and Edward Bigelow, Sausalito, California.

All photographs of works by Art Grant and Henry Rasmusen, except where credited otherwise, were taken by the latter.

Frontispiece. Watts Towers (detail) by Simon Rodia. (Photograph by Elaine Mayes.)

© 1967, Art Horizons, Inc.
All rights reserved
Printed in the United States of America
Library of Congress Catalog Card Number: 67-14160
Design Consultant: Milton Glaser
Type set by Graphic Arts Typographers, Inc.
Printed by New York Lithographing Corp.
Bound by William Marley Co.
Published by Reinhold Publishing Corporation
A subsidiary of Chapman-Reinhold, Inc.
430 Park Avenue, New York, N.Y. 10022

4

Contents

Venus of Willendorf. Prehistoric fertility figure from southern Austria. (Collection Naturhistorisches Museum, Vienna.)

Introduction

The word "Junk" in the title of this book is employed in a broad and liberal sense, including not only those things which have been used and discarded by man, but also unused alter-purpose items—made for one purpose and adapted to another, and found nature-objects such as stones, shells, beachwood and the like.

The twentieth-century art revolution, starting with the introduction of collage by the Cubists and continuing through Dada and up to Pop Art, brought the use of unorthodox materials in the visual arts into general acceptance. The use of unconventional materials offers the artist several important premiums. Discarded or found objects often suggest the form and theme for a work of art, and by doing a little carving, or by adding other odds and ends, the artist can produce an interesting and unusual piece.

In junk sculpturing the finished product appears sooner and more directly from the heat of expression because the materials are already of a permanent nature and do not require casting, firing, or re-carving. Also, because the parts are already more or less fully formed, they can easily be held or placed next to each other temporarily to get a visual idea of the completed composition before final bonding

Lastly, the tools required are few and the materials are plentiful and free. These features make sculpturing from junk attractive not only to professionals, but to amateurs and children as well, bringing them into an activity where worthwhile results are obtained almost at once, allowing a feeling of accomplishment at each step in the perfection of the craft.

1.
A Brief History

From prehistoric times man has collected and used the found or discarded objects of his environment—hair, feathers, bones, shells, and pebbles. Recent primitive tribes have added to these a variety of discards from the more sophisticated societies—cans, bottles, rope, string, plastics, and other things.

It is probable that early man's first attempts at figurative sculpture were the result of finding rocks, bones, and pieces of wood in which heads and bodies of human or animal forms were already suggested, so that it was necessary only to clarify the image with a small amount of carving.

Many artists in Europe and America from the sixteenth century to today have painted still lifes from pre-arranged collage or assemblage set-ups. During the last century and the beginning of this one folk artists made constructions from flowers, hair, buttons, stamps, and shells, and displayed them in frames and glass bells for friends and relatives to enjoy.

Among professionals, Picasso, in his Cubist painting *Still Life with Chair Caning*, 1911, is credited with being the first to incorporate actual found objects in a picture. During the same year the Futurist, Boccioni, made a three-dimensional construction, *Fusion of a Head and Window*, of plaster and wood discards.

After 1913, Picasso, Braque, and Gris often included scraps of newspaper, wallpaper, and other printed matter in their Cubist works. Up to recent times Picasso intermittently continued to make constructions and bronze castings from found objects, carrying out his wish to "debunk the idea of 'noble' means," as he put it.

The champion debunkers, the Dadaists, used combine-paintings, ready-mades, collages, and assemblages as their weapons against the sentimental and pompous in art and life. The Surrealists, noting the ironic symbology inherent in the medium, juxtaposed strange and incongruous subjects to suggest new and oftentimes weird meanings. Picabia, Balla, Duchamp, Arp, Ernst, Man Ray and Breton are some of the foremost names of the period.

About the same time, just before and during the nineteen-twenties, the German Kurt Schwitters explored the assemblage medium, making outstanding contributions to art, anticipating even the most recent developments.

For two decades after the twenties a small number of talented people worked seriously in the medium. Among these were Joseph Cornell and the folk artist Simon Rodia. Also, Joan Miro, Max Ernst, Man Ray, and a few other Dadaists and Surrealists continued working with discards to some extent.

In the fifties junk sculpturing enjoyed a big resurgence in the work of the Neo-Dadaists. The Pop Artists added impetus to this revival during the sixties. Inside and outside these movements the works of Nevelson, Dubuffet, Tinguely, Seley, Rauschenberg, Johns, Burri, Cézar, Stankiewicz, Oldenberg, Dine, Mallary and Kienholz are outstanding examples of the creative use of discards.

Baboon and Young by Pablo Picasso.
Bronze. (Collection The Museum of
Modern Art, New York, Mrs. Simon
Guggenheim Fund.)

The Centimeters 1918 by Francis Picabia.
Collage and oil on canvas.
(Galleria Schwarz, Milan.)

Guitar and Wine Glass 1913 by Pablo
Picasso. (Collection Marion Koogler
McNay Art Institute, San Antonio,
Texas.)

Ready-Made, Why Not Sneeze Rose Selavy? 1921 by Marcel Duchamp. (Collection Philadelphia Museum of Art. Photograph by A.J. Wyatt.)

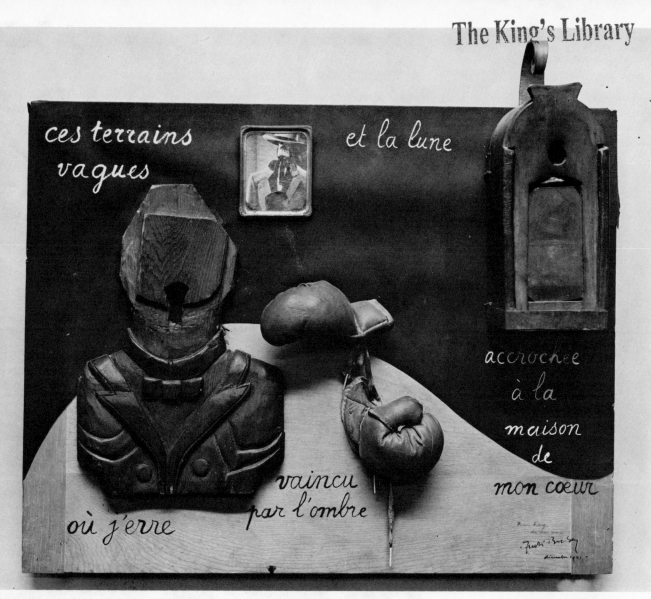

ces terrains vagues
et la lune
accrochée à la maison de mon cœur
où j'erre
vaincu par l'ombre

Opposite Page
Two Heads 1927 by Jean (Hans) Arp.
Oil and string on canvas. (Collection
The Museum of Modern Art, New
York.)

Objet Poeme by André Breton.
Assemblage: carved wood bust of
man, wood and metal lantern,
photograph in metal frame, toy
boxing gloves, mounted on wood board
and black paper with inscription
painted in gouache and oil. (Collection
The Museum of Modern Art, New
York, Kay Sage Tanguy Bequest.)

Watts Towers (detail) by Simon
Rodia. Concrete and iron, embellished
with glass, tiles, shells, etc.
(Photograph by Ralph Gibson.)

Chant du Nightingale by Joseph Cornell. Found objects, including stamps and coins. (Allen Stone Galleries, New York.)

Dawn's Wedding Feast (detail) by
Louise Nevelson. White wood.
(Martha Jackson Gallery, New York.
Photograph by Rudolph Burckhardt.)

18

The Lamp Shade by Seymour Locks.
(Photograph by Jack Welpott.)

Untitled by Richard Stankiewicz.
Steel. (Collection Mr. and Mrs. Burton
Tremaine, Meriden, Connecticut.)

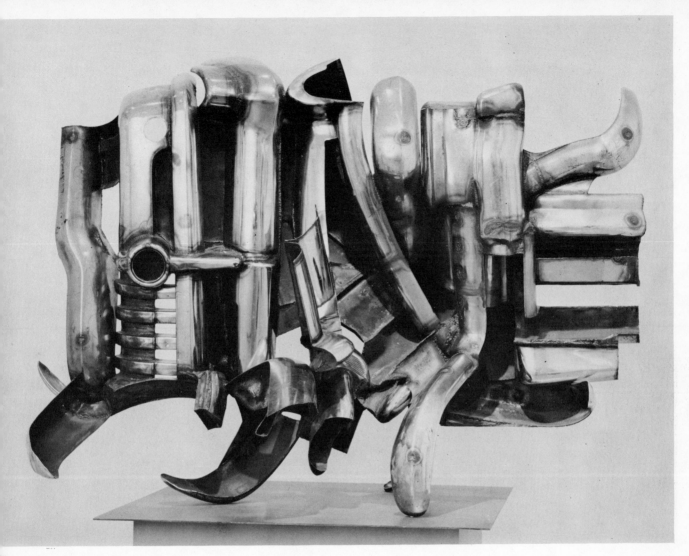

The Boys from Avignon by Jason
Seley. Automobile bumpers. (Kornblee
Gallery, New York. Photograph by
Charles Uht.)

The Beanery by Edward Kienholz.
Mixed media tableau. (Dwan Gallery,
Los Angeles.)

2.
Approach

There are three basic steps to keep in mind when making junk sculpture. First—and it will probably take some practice—is *slowing down and looking*. This is important because a sensitive awareness of the visual elements of color, shape, line, and texture in natural and man-made objects is essential in making sculptures. Second is *finding the materials*. Third is *creating the sculpture*.

Regarding the first step, *slowing down and looking*, there is much that can be said. Most people look without really seeing. Full, perceptive awareness comes only after a great deal of quiet observation, comparing, and sensing. One must slow down and look with the wide-eyed wonder of a child.

For practice in visual perception the following method is suggested. It was developed for groups of students as part of a program of sensory awareness, but the individual can easily do it by himself or with another person or two: A slow walk is taken through a park or wooded area. A particular shrub or tree is chosen and fifteen minutes or more is spent in examining the various aspects of it—its overall shape, the character of its limbs, the color and texture of its bark, the shape and quality of its leaves. Noted are the way the roots follow a rhythmic course of growth, also the fact that the thousands of leaves have common family traits yet no two are exactly alike. Attention is given to any patterns caused by saw-cuts or natural breakage, and the designs made by insects and birds, as well as any

natural growths such as moss or fungus. Any decayed parts are studied for their color, structure, and general appearance.

Comparisons are made with other senses as well : touch, smell—even taste. After investigating the characteristics of the one tree the same procedure is followed with others, and also grasses, insects, rocks, dirt and other things encountered during the walk.

As soon as one begins to be aware of the visual world he is then ready to begin the second step, *finding the materials* for sculptural use.

An artist of today has few limitations regarding the types of materials and techniques available. Besides such traditional media as oil paints and canvas, clay and stone, he is free to use anything that pleases his fancy—burlap, mirrors, charred wood, rusted metals, plastics, magazine clippings, photographs, just about anything—from the familiar to the exotic—that will stay put.

The present technological age makes available countless discarded parts of manufactured goods such as television and radio sets, automobiles, bicycles, washing machines, electrical gadgets, as well as cans, bottles, and other things. For attaching and assembling, there is a profusion of new synthetic plastics, glues, and cements.

The novice must realize that artistic quality has nothing to do with cost, polish, status value, prettiness, or even cleanliness. Often, things considered ugly, such as rust or corrosion, possess great

beauty, for deterioration and fragmentation lend visual variety and richness to materials and objects.

Imagination and inventiveness are two essentials that the junk sculptor should develop. Everyone has at one time or another found images in such things as rocks, wood grain, clouds, and mountain peaks. The artist using discards makes a habit of seeing images in natural and man-made objects. Upon finding an article in which a subject is suggested, he uses his imagination to bring the partially formed idea into fulfillment.

Practice in seeing images in things can begin around the house, or while taking a walk through the town where one lives. Man's unconscious feeling for balance and symmetry causes many of the gadgets he makes to look like human faces and figures. For manufactured goods one might take a tour through a hardware store or a salvage shop. It will be seen that various tools suggest animals or humans—a saw handle looks like a horse's head, an upturned paint brush like a man's head with hair on end, and a pair of house jacks look like soldiers or guards standing at attention.

The places to search for sculptural materials, of course, are wherever one is apt to find discards—in drawers, cupboards, gutters, attics, basements, backyards, alleys, and dumps. Natural or organic materials such as wood and stones are most likely to be found along rivers and beaches, forests and mountains, and in the deserts. Often a piece may be found

Stump. (Photograph by Frank Mulvey.)

Eroded rock. (Photograph by Frank Mulvey.)

which suggests no particular figurative image, but is coveted as a thing of pure abstract beauty.

There is an honesty to be observed with materials. Each type—wood, metal, plastic, or other—has its own peculiar qualities and characteristics which should be honored and enhanced. Attempting to cover up or change the surface of one material to make it appear like something else is defeating of the junk sculptor's purpose. In this medium, where much of the charm results from the eroded and patinated surfaces of both natural and man-made materials, it is to the artist's advantage to accept and nurture these qualities.

Rock formations, Goblin Valley, Utah. (Photograph by Hal Rumel.)

House jacks. Objects found by
Eleanor Dickenson. (Photograph by
Warner Jepson.)

Opposite Page
Figures and faces everywhere.
(Photographs by Henry Rasmusen.)

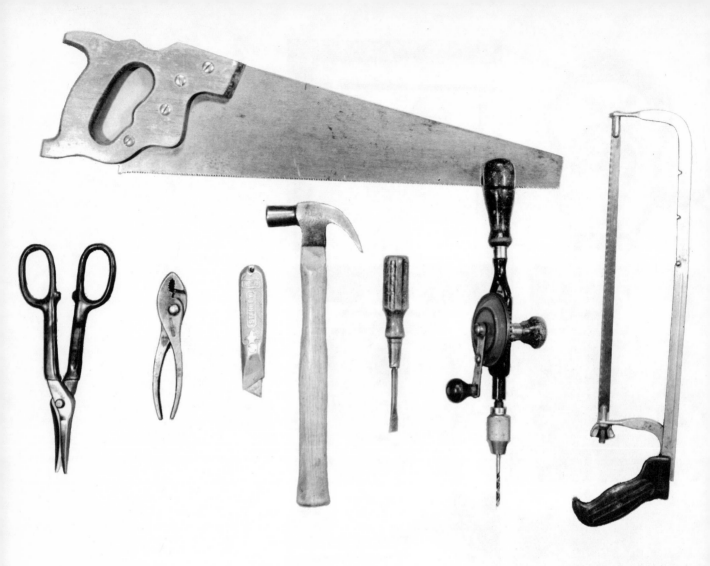

Basic tools needed: wood saw, tin
snips, pliers, carpenter's utility knife,
hammer, screwdriver, hand drill, and
hack saw.

3.
Materials, Composition, and Finishing

TOOLS AND BONDING MATERIALS

The beginner needs very few tools for junk sculpturing, mainly the eight basic ones illustrated here. Later he may want to go into some heavier equipment such as electric saws and drills. These save time and effort but do not necessarily improve the quality of the work.

The carpenter's utility knife is the primary tool used for whittling. In it one should use heavy-duty blades. For carving larger pieces or very hard woods, a chisel, gouge, and axe are a help.

Each kind and weight of material requires a different type of adherent or hardware. A heavy metal, for instance, may require drilling holes and attaching with bolts or wire, while a thinner, lighter material like paper may need only some sort of water-base glue. Special glues and cements are made for particular materials such as wood, paper, plastic, metal, and glass. Following are descriptions of a few of the basic ones:

White Glue. Especially good for thin, light materials like paper, cardboard, cloth and leather. Also bonds wood, Masonite, asphalt, linoleum, pottery, glass, plaster and polystyrene. Produces a strong shock-resistant joint. Sets rapidly; woodworking operations can be performed twenty minutes after gluing. Will not crystallize. Spreads easily, dries colorless and is weather-resistant. Sold under various trade names: *Elmer's Glue, Flexweld, Glu Bird, Wilhold White Glue,* etc.

Lacquer Cement. For use on glass, pottery, leather, fabrics, metal, wood, and paper products. A fast drying, transparent, general purpose, waterproof cement. Not affected by heat, cold, or moisture. Trade names: *Duco, Testor's Household Cement,* etc.

Epoxy Glue. Binds almost anything to anything: metal, wood, brick, concrete, stone, glass, plastic, and so on. Makes a hard, waterproof, heat-resistant bond which stands the test of time and remains immune to practically all materials and forces. Dries in six to eight hours; reaches maximum strength in three days. Trade names: *Carters, Boxer Epoxy, Wilhold,* etc.

Epoxy Putty. Reinforced with metals. Similar to epoxy glue, but more dense. Can be molded, drilled, sawed, filed, sanded, threaded, and painted. Trade names: *Epoxybond, Wilhold,* etc.

Oxy-Acetylene Welding. The beginner probably will not encounter a problem in which heavy or large metal sculptures call for welding. If he does, there are usually professional welders in the community who can do the job under his supervision. Later on, for more advanced work, he may decide to learn the technique of welding himself.

Wire. The junk sculptor should have a few feet of strong, flexible wire of various weights on hand for assembling art works. Gauges 12, 16, and 20 are most often used.

COMPOSITION

The ways of achieving unity in art works are almost as varied as the number of artists producing them. However, the visual elements of line, tone-value, shape, color, and texture are the basic constants used by all artists in composing a visual work of art. The following examples show how these may be rhymed, repeated and balanced in a number of ways to bring order and variety to the whole.

MOUNTING AND FINISHING

There are three general ways to mount a sculpture: on a base, hanging or protruding from a wall, or hanging from a ceiling.

Many pieces will stand by themselves and do not require a base. Others, if in a single unit, call for some sort of base wide or heavy enough to hold the object up without its toppling over. The material can be of the same type as the figure to be mounted, or of a different kind that is harmonious with it and at the same time slightly complementary to it in color, tone, shape, and texture.

The correct height of a base is important; some pieces need a tall one while others require a medium or short one. One of the first things to do when mounting a work is to view it from different angles and levels, so that its best side can be dramatized with the most appropriate base.

In finishing, the ideal is for the object and its parts to possess a richness and unity of color, tone, and texture in their natural state so that no surface coating or treating is necessary. When this is not possible it may be painted, stained, varnished, or waxed.

Arteriosclerosis by Arman. (Galleria
Schwarz, Milan.) This assemblage
seems to have been produced by
letting knives and forks fall
haphazardly, arranging themselves
by chance, which in this instance
works very well. In spite of the
complexity of numbers, it holds
together because of the close similarity
of all the shapes, the small differences
between fork prongs and spoon bowls
lending some variety.

Below. Big Mouth, Little Man
by Art Grant. The repetition of
cylindrical shapes of head, body,
eyes and nose produces a simple,
unified statement, the mouth echoing
the rectangular shape of the cylinder
chest as it appears from the side.

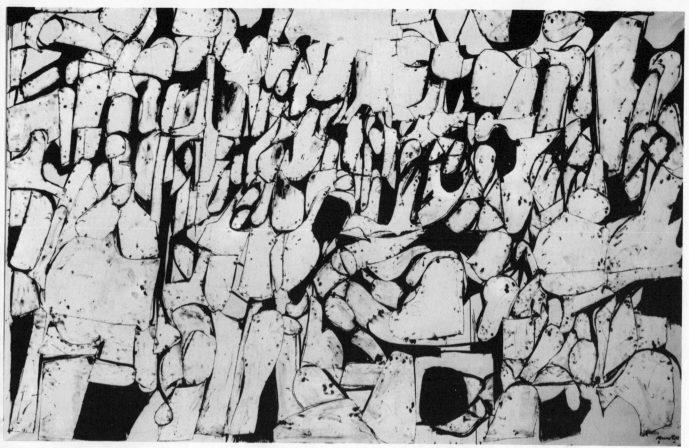

Trial by Marca-Relli. (Collection
The Minneapolis Institute of Arts,
Julia B. Bigelow Fund.) Strongly
contrasting tones of near black and
white emphasize the dovetailed
patterns in this striking composition.
Large shapes are played against
smaller ones; dots and lines are
repeated and varied to create
cohesiveness and subtle variety.

Icon to Nyla Marie by Mel Hanson. (The Green Gallery, San Francisco.) Through a symmetrical arrangement of three panels and cupola this Pop Art assemblage attains a classical balance. The smaller shapes of doll heads and bodies pressed tightly together inside the boxed sections contribute texture and scale which contrast with the larger rectangles and total shape.

Opposite Page
Bonnie Prince Stuart by Tony Berlant. (Collection Mr. and Mrs. David Stuart, Los Angeles.) In this charming work the repetition of round-headed bolts holds the composition together, as they literally do, physically. Added to that are the rhythms of line and contour which lead the eye to the child's face, natural focal point of the picture.

Bones No. 14 by Robert McChesney. Here the symmetrical balance is relieved by off-centering the two large ovals and by the changes of shape, weight, and color of the forms at the left and right sides at middle, top, and bottom. The light tones of the bones and metal strapping contrast nicely with the darker background, as do the delicate bones opposed to the heavier ones.

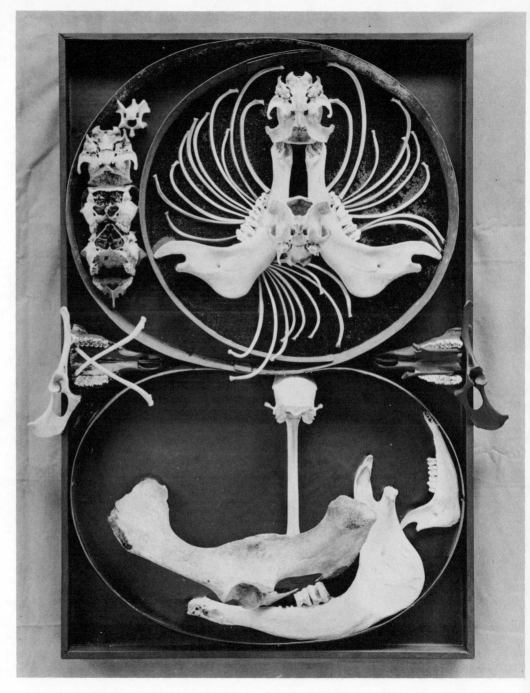

Merzbilde med regnbue by Kurt
Schwitters. (The Estate of Kurt
Schwitters, Courtesy Marlborough-
Gerson Gallery, New York.)

Fountain by Art Grant. A found object may be developed in several different ways. *Fountain* was created from a washing machine agitator.

Opposite Page
Above. Object by Joan Miro. (Philadelphia Museum of Art, A. E. Gallatin Collection.) Miro illustrates unusual imagination in assembling and in finishing by painting designs on the rock.

Below. Rhinoceros by Anne Arnold. (Collection Mr. Edward Bragsline.) Constructed from discarded slabs of pine logs. The surface was first bleached and then slightly stained and varnished to preserve the natural color of the wood.

Monument by Henry Rasmusen. Example of objects being left in their natural state, balancing surface tones and textures against each other.

Le Folatre by Jean Dubuffet. (Collection Mr. and Mrs. Harry Lewis Winston, Birmingham, Michigan.) Some sculptures need no base. Here, just a bit of cement was added to give the figure something flat to rest on.

Vulnerable by Sadie Hayms. Created from car grills and windshield wipers. For this kind of unique, textured finish the artist uses an acrylic resin in which various things are added, such as asbestos, sand, marble dust, or vermiculite, plus dry pigments for coloration. Several coats are applied to create heavier textures.

al Tide IV by Louise Nevelson.
artha Jackson Gallery, New York.)
other method of mounting. The
ed units are complete compositions
hemselves and together form an
over design. Everything was
ded to give a uniform effect to the
glomerate discards.

41

Owls by Art Grant. Heavy pulleys
and a metal box were used for bases.

42

Jewelry from carved driftwood by Mary Lou Stribbling. A more complicated finish. After the shapes were developed from found beach bark and driftwood, the pendant was burnished with a steel brush to remove spongy strata, then sealed with low-gloss varnish. A wash of moss green polymer paint was applied to high spots and several chunks of Dioptase, a turquoise colored material, were set in the crevices. The brooch was gold-leafed, then dark, transparent pigments were used to antique the leaf.

Below. Which Way's the Moat? by Maxine Fiaccadori. (Photograph by John Grant.) Surfaces unified by spraying with flat black enamel.

4.
Techniques

WHITTLING AND CARVING

Found tree branches and roots have a liveliness, symmetry, and rhythm that are often suggestive of the human or animal form. With a little practice these partial or suggestive images can be released by whittling away extraneous parts to create a sculpture of a head, a bust, or a body.

The trick is to carve as simply and directly as possible, stopping just at the point where the image is clearly defined, avoiding an overworked appearance, and taking advantage of the natural weathered quality of the original wood. In carving, the freshly cut inside tone and color will appear. These new surfaces can be played against the contrasting weathered surfaces when the artist becomes sensitive to them.

The grain, bark, knots, and holes, as well as the shape and action of the original piece, all give indications of what the result might be and the procedure for achieving it. Generally speaking, the wood should be solid and sound. Rotted pieces are impossible to carve and quite impermanent for works of art.

If a chunk is cut off by mistake it can be glued on again with lacquer cement, the carving proceeding as soon as it is dry.

To avoid accidents care should be taken to push the knife away from the hand or body. For extra safety a leather glove can be worn on the hand that holds the wood. Cutting can be controlled by gripping the knife firmly with one hand and pushing it with the thumb of the other.

Cupboard of figures and heads carved from furniture parts and other objects by Art Grant.

45

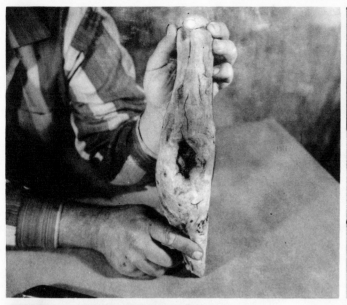

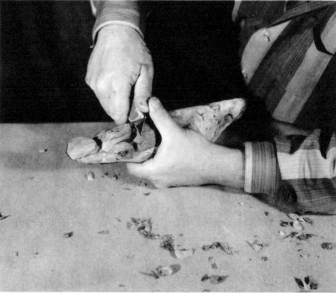

1
Above. Piece of driftwood is examined
for suggested image.

3
Below. Whittling continues with
carving of arms and hands.

2
Above. After deciding on a female
figure, head and breasts are carved,
taking advantage of knots.

4
Below. Figure is studied for final
touch up.

46

Above. Extermination Camp.

Below. Four Dancers by Art Grant.

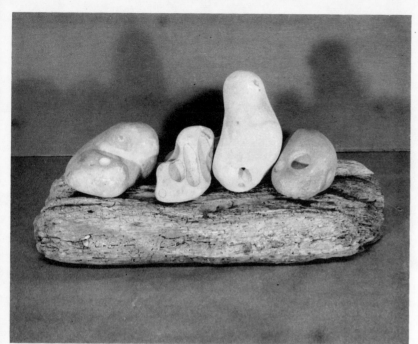

Above. Family.
Below. Bust.

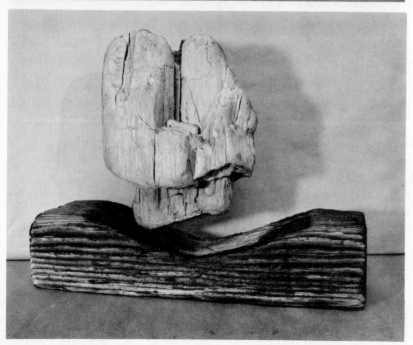

49

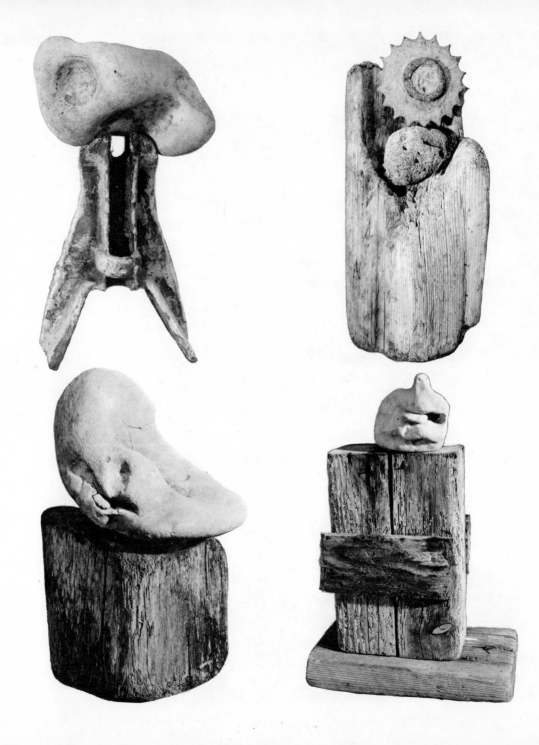

Left. Self Portrait.
Right. Angel.

Left. Found Stone No. 1.
Right. Monument to Phfft!

51

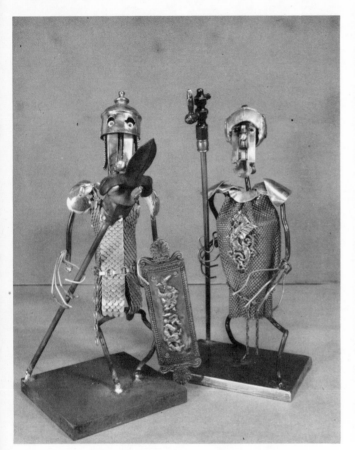

Willie and Joe, c. 1006 A. D. by Donald Crist.
Metallic mesh purse and belt, necklaces,
drapery-bar furrel, earrings, and other objects.

Head of Girl by Bernice Kussoy.
Bicycle chains, metal
washers, bolts, etc.

Compression Dirigee A by Cesar.
Compressed copper automobile parts.
(Saidenberg Gallery, New York.)

Progress Junk by Fred Sauls. Farm
machinery parts and shovel.
(Photograph courtesy *Artforum.*)

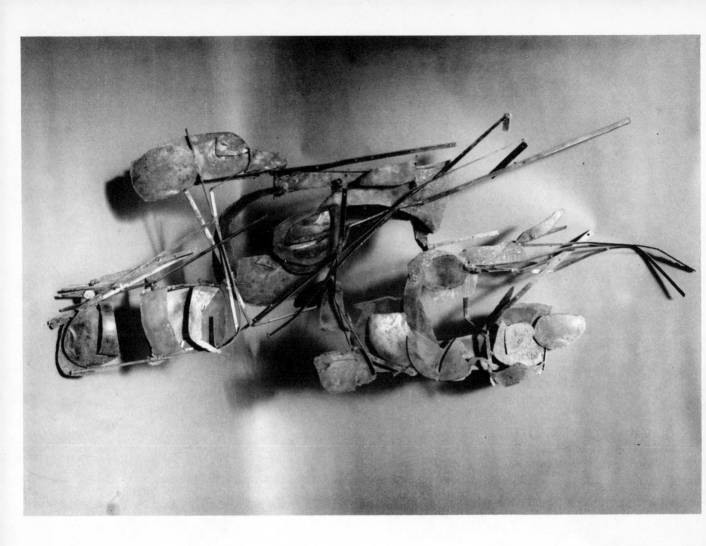

Sea Grass by Shirley Rousseau-Murphey. 48 by 144 inches. Forms cut from automobile body parts. (Collection Mr. and Mrs. Henry Rasmusen.)

Below. Steam Trumpet by Jack Hoag. Brass and copper plumbing parts. Steam generated in boiler activates reeds and whistles in various nozzles. (Collection Oakland Art Museum.)

Little Red Devil. Paint scraper, hinge,
fan pump, and part of music stand.

Jardin des Isles by Jean Dubuffet.
(Collection Pomona College Gallery,
Claremont, California, Gift of Norton Simon.)

Top. The artist gathers together several stove legs, one of which suggests an elephant's head.

Center. Four stove legs are bolted together to form the body and legs of the elephant.

Bottom. After drilling holes for eyes, the artist places bolts in them and attaches the head to the body.

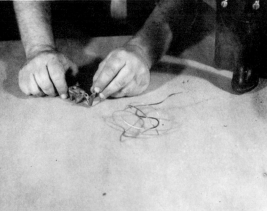

Top. An electric iron thermostat dial and a rope or cable clamp make a small elephant.

Center. A small clamp and metal clip make a baby elephant.

Bottom. Papa and Baby Elephants by Art Grant.

Holy Woman. Stove decoration, sugar tongs. grass clippers, and automobile part. (Photograph by Ray Anderson.)

Mama, Papa and Baby. Coffee pots and urns.

Man. Motorcycle and automobile parts.

Giraffes. Stove legs, gas burner, ladle, frying pan and hinges.

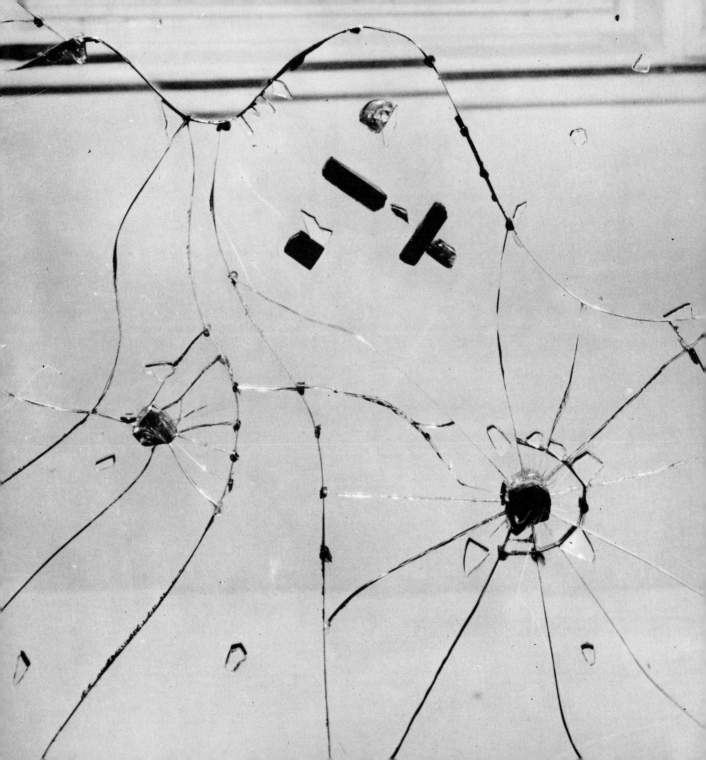

Above. Head by Art Grant. Plastic
bleach bottle and light socket.

Right. Untitled Sculpture by Lucas
Samaras. (Pace Gallery, New York.)

Opposite Page
Mirror by Enrico Baj. Broken mirror
on brocade fabric. (Galleria Schwarz,
Milan.)

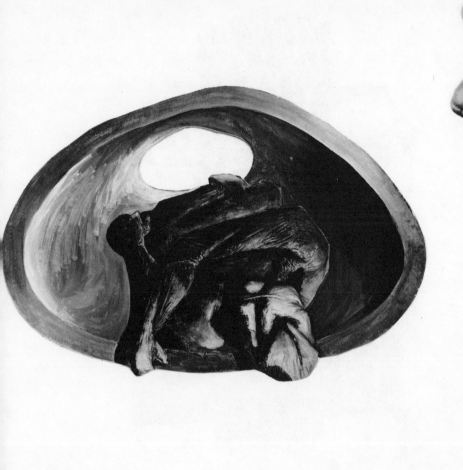

Above. The Tube by Leonard Breger.
Stuffed rags mounted on painted
panel. (Photograph by Fred Ross.)

Right. The Long Arm of the Law
by Michael Todd. Artificial leg, hand,
and other objects. (Pace Gallery,
New York.)

Opposite Page
Portuguese Man of War by Knute
Stiles. Chains, cords, beads, and
buttons on fabric. (Photograph by
Joe Humphrey.)

Portrait of George Herms by Bruce Conner. Wood, letters, cork, etc. (Photograph by Wayne Sourbeer.)

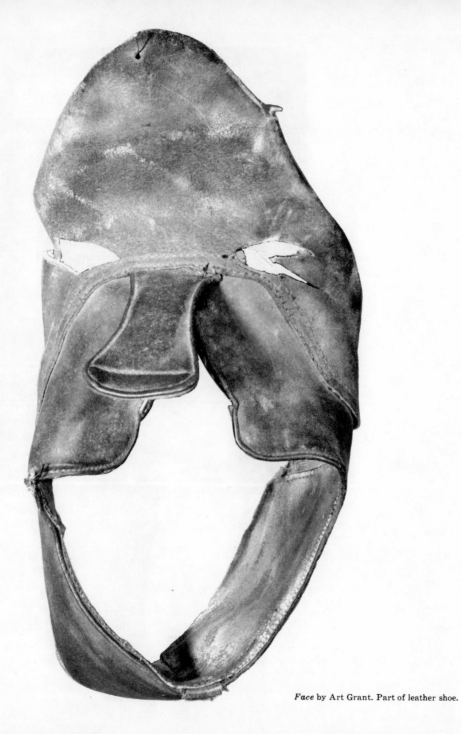

Face by Art Grant. Part of leather shoe.

The Perfect Dart Board by George
Herms. (Collection Los Angeles
County Museum of Art.)

Little Hans by Robert Mallary.
Tuxedo and polyester. (Allan Stone
Galleries, New York.)

Essex by John Chamberlain.
Automobile body parts and other
metal, relief. (Collection The Museum
of Modern Art, New York. Gift of
Mr. and Mrs. Robert C. Scull and
purchase fund.)

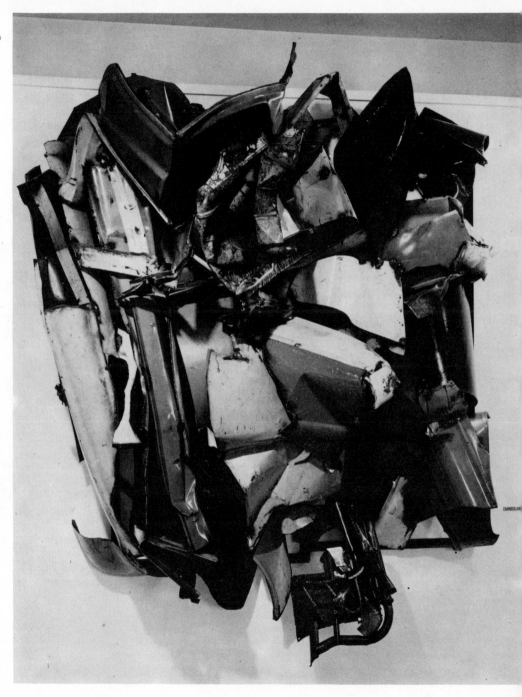

Winter Wall by Peter Agostini.
Fabric and plaster on wood. (Stephen
Radich Gallery, New York.)

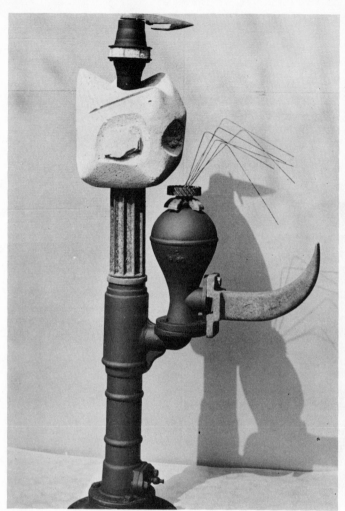

Arizona, Mon Amour by Mary Fuller.
Scrap metal and concrete.

Ominous Event by Harry Crotty.
Tire retread rasp wheels, automobile
oil pan, etc.

Y'Everting Vun by Stanley Moskowitz. Milk cartons, paper cups, plastic bottles, toys and other objects covered with layers of pasted paper.

Sexagon by Bill Snyder. Manikin, plastered and painted, fur, fruit box, table legs. (Green Gallery, San Francisco. Photograph by Donald Hugh Bennett.)

Rope and People by Joan Miro. Oil on cardboard with coil of rope. (Collection The Museum of Modern Art, New York.)

Kichka's Breakfast No. 2 by Daniel
Spoerri. (Galleria Schwarz, Milan.)

The Strong Man by Lino Pera.
(Photograph by Michael Bry.)

MOBILES AND KINETIC SCULPTURE

Perhaps no art forms are more expressive
of the twentieth century than mobiles and
kinetic sculptures, reflecting as they do
the modern scientific concepts of space,
energy, and matter in motion. Earlier, in
the nineteenth century, there was the
activated machinery of the workaday
world—clocks, windmills, factory
machines, steam engines, dynamos, and
other mechanical inventions of the
Industrial Revolution.

The precursors of mobile artists were
painters, beginning with the
Impressionists, who broke the world into
tiny fragments of color. Next, the Cubists
fractured the solid and reassembled it,
followed by the Futurists who sought to
introduce the element of movement to
painting and sculpture.

In all of these motion was more
suggested than real. It was the American
artist, Alexander Calder, who released
sculpture from its traditional bounds with
the creation of the mobile, so delicately
balanced that it moves at the touch of a
finger or a tiny gust of wind.

Following this was kinetic sculpture,
activated by motors and other mechanical
means. Finally, perhaps symbolically
suggesting that art forms and trends
follow a cycle of birth, growth, and death,
we have self-creating and self-destroying
sculptures.

Constellation
by Henry Rasmusen.
Wood and wire.

Opposite Page
Hanging Sculpture by Art Grant.
Wire rack and wire. (Photograph by
Glenn E. Mitchell.)

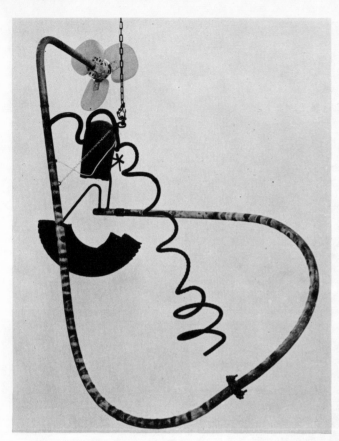

Love Is Just a Flower by Seccombe.
Welded steel with tire. Fan driven;
winds and unwinds every 20 minutes.

By Hook or by Crook II by Jean
Tinguely. Motorized iron. (Alexander
Iolas Gallery, New York.)

Sun Cart by Oliver Andrews.
Bronze, wood, and iron.

The A Train by Mark di Suvero.
Wood and steel. (Park Place Gallery,
New York.)

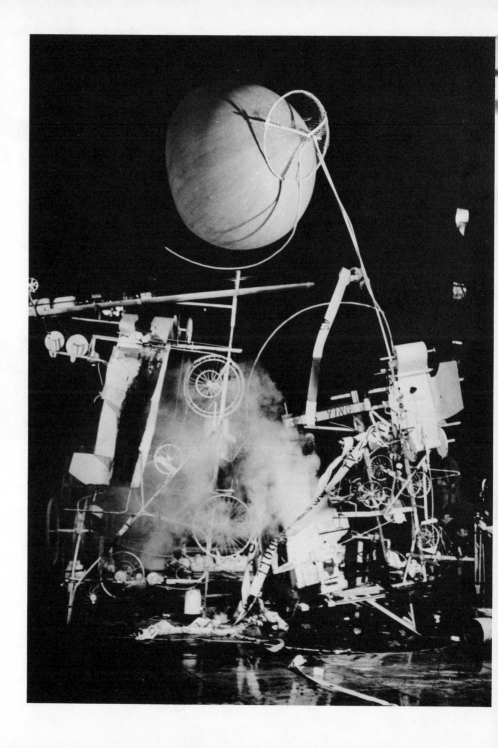

oltergeist by Seccombe.
Welded steel with tire.
an driven; winds and un-
inds every 20 minutes.

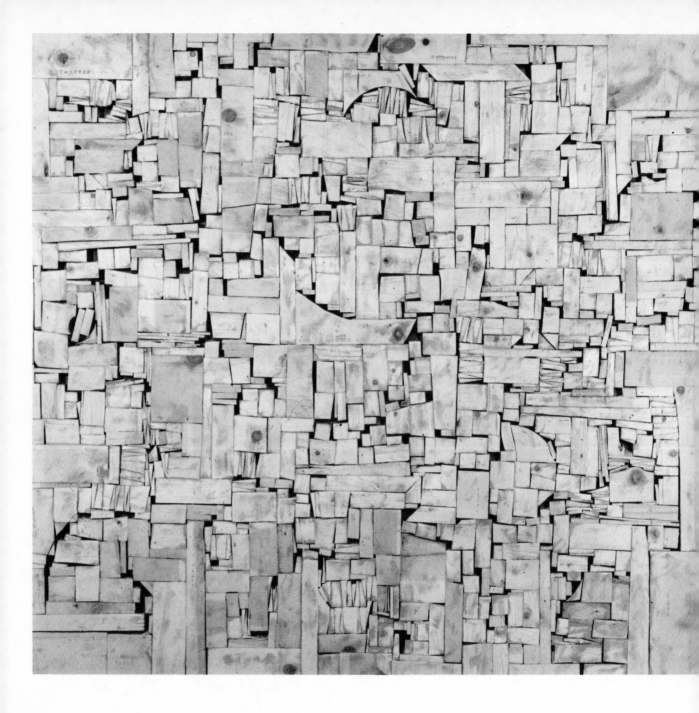

82

MOSAICS AND INTARSIA

A mosaic may be framed and hung like a painting, used as a table or counter top or as a decorative or structural motif on a house or other building.

After gathering the bits and parts from which the mosaic will be made they can be arranged and glued spontaneously, or a careful preliminary sketch may be made before starting. The parts are usually bonded to a panel of Masonite or plywood with white glue.

In conventional mosaics, especially where a relatively flat surface is desired, a thick cement called "grout" is filled in between the pieces. Depending on the material used and the purpose to which the work will be put, this is not always desirable. The term *intarsia* is used when small pieces of wood are fitted together.

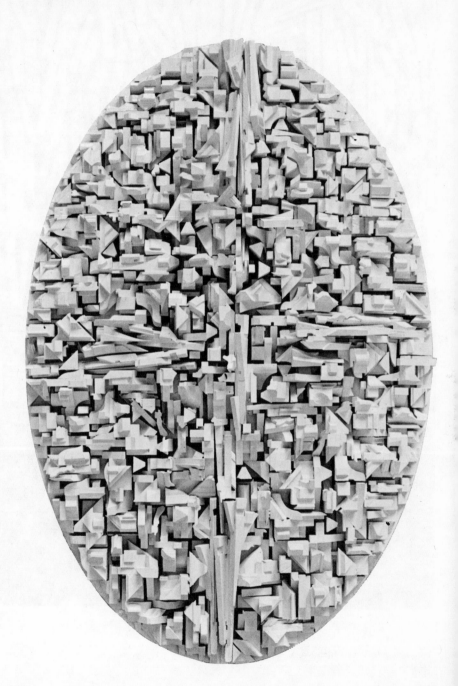

Oval (metric series) by Faralla. Wood painted white. (Collection San Francisco Museum of Art.)

Opposite Page
Plan with Blue by Bernard Langlais. (Allan Stone Galleries, New York.) These two examples, and that on the following page, show three different approaches to the use of wood scraps in tarsia assemblage.

Yellow Bush by Robert Biancalana.
Painted, weathered wood.

84

Praying Mantis by Helen Steineau
Rich. (Collection Mrs. Edgar Sinton.)
Conventional tesserae combined with
found beach pebbles, abalone shell,
and scraps of discarded metal.

Mosaic mural (detail) by Emmy Lou
Packard. Hillcrest Elementary School,
San Francisco. Detail of large mosaic
mural executed by 650 elementary
school children under the artist's
direction. The project took 27 days
to complete. No grout was used.

Top. Pendants from found stones by
Frieda Burkhart. Left to right:
cathedral crystals, azurite and
malachite, and malachite.

Center. Necklace by Art Grant. Parts from radio tubes.

Bottom. Necklace by Anne R. Dick. Hot metal droppings.

Opposite Page
Earring by Art Grant. Hair clip.
(Modeled by Tye Rasmusen.)

Portrait of Ralph Dusenberry by
Arthur G. Dove. Oil on canvas with
applied wood and paper. (The
Metropolitan Museum of Art, New
York, The Alfred Stieglitz Collection.)

Opposite Page
Collage and Oil by Jackson Pollock.
(The Joseph H. Hirshhorn
Foundation, New York.)

COLLAGE

Collage is the art of pasting objects on a relatively flat plane. As the plane approaches greater depth the term "assemblage" or "construction" is usually applied.

In collage the materials are generally thin and lightweight, like paper, cardboard, leather, cloth, and plastic. Often these are discards of printed materials—newspapers, magazines, posters, stamps, tickets, fabrics, and similar things that possess a variety of simulated textures and subjective meanings.

The relative simplicity of the two-dimensional plane, plus the ease of adjusting and perfecting a design before final adhering, makes collage an advantageous medium, popular with young and old alike. Following are several collage methods:

Collage combine: Combining of pasting techniques with those of drawing, painting, or sculpture.

Creasing: Folding, crushing, or crumbling of materials.

Cutting: Hard edge cutting with scissors, razor blade, or other tool.

Montage: Combining of pictorial elements from a number of sources in a way that retains the identity of individual parts while forming an overall composition.

Offset textures: Patterns left by wet paint. These can be purposely produced by applying paint to a surface, pressing a piece of paper onto it, and pulling it off.

Rubbing: Transferring a design or texture from a relief surface, such as in placing a piece of paper over a coin and rubbing the top with a crayon or pencil.

Scorching: Burning or scorching the edges of paper, cloth, and other material, after which it is pasted down. When dry, the charred surfaces are lightly rubbed with fine steel wool.

Scraping: Scratching or scraping a surface to create textures and patterns.

Smoking: Creating tones and patterns by smoking the surface of a material by

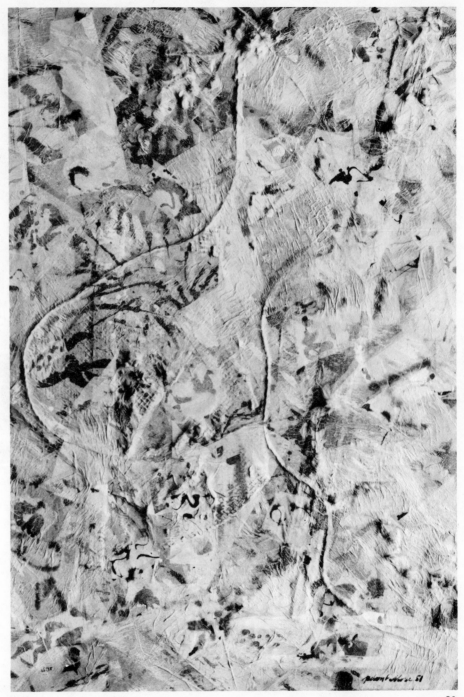

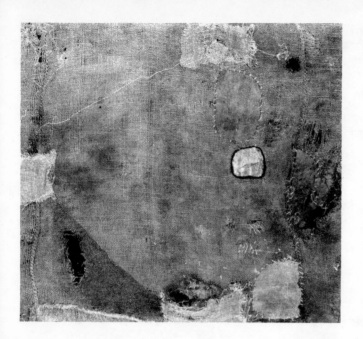

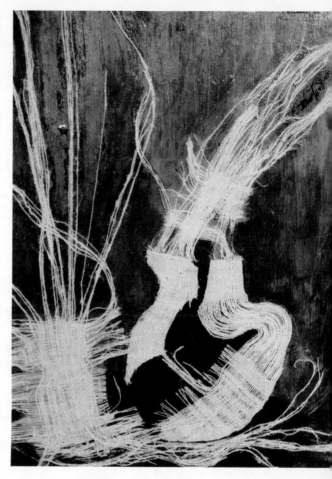

holding it over a flame.

Stripping: Detaching or peeling of
previously dried materials.

Tearing wet paper: A different effect from
dry paper.

Torn edges: Usually thin paper products.
Tearing produces a rougher, more varied
edge than cutting.

Unaltered materials: Use of such things
as stamps, letters, and posters unaltered
from their original found condition.

Unsticking: Ungluing of partially
adhered materials, leaving fragments still
attached.

Left. Queen of Cities: Aerial View by
Robert Collins. Collage, acrylic, and oil.

Right. No. 10, 1957 by Esteban Vicente.
(Andre Emmerich Gallery, New
York.)

Opposite Page
Left. Composition 8 by Alberto Burri.
Burlap sewn, patched and glued over
canvas. (Collection The Museum of
Modern Art, New York, Mr. and Mrs.
David M. Solinger Fund.)

Right. Still Life with Jug by Elvie Ten
Moor. Leather and burlap on Masonite.

PRINTMAKING FROM DISCARDS

The collage technique is only one step away from that of making collagraphs, etchings using textured materials, and certain kinds of monotypes wherein a collage-type plate is constructed.

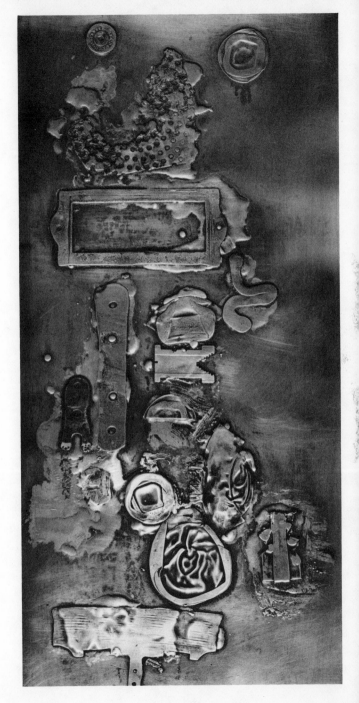

Photograph of the original plate for the collagraph, *Emeryville*, by Daniel Shapiro. Brass, copper and steel discards were soldered for making collagraphic prints.

Opposite Page
Collagraph No. 1 by John Kalamaras. Sometimes the objects are not glued down but are inked and printed individually in progressive stages. Automobile gaskets and transmission parts, zinc sheets, heavy canvas, and other objects were used here.

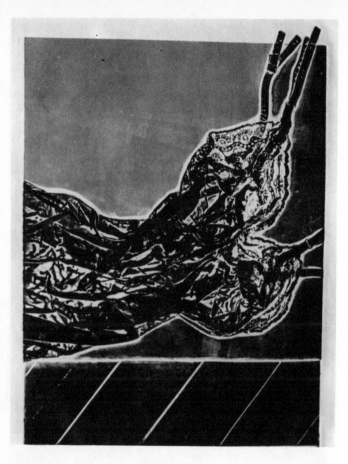

High Wind by Karl Kasten. Collagraph. In collatype the relatively flat objects are glued onto a piece of Masonite, then lithographer's or printer's ink is applied, after which it is run through an etching press. Here, the discarded objects were a woman's underslip and a flattened cardboard paper-towel tube.

Ancient Arboretum in Winter by Gordon W. Gilkey. Soft-ground etching. This print was produced by arranging wood fragments and cellophane on a copper plate covered with soft etcher's ground, after which it was run through a press, making an impression in the soft ground. The discards were then removed and the plate placed in acid and bitten in the usual way, after which it was inked and printed.

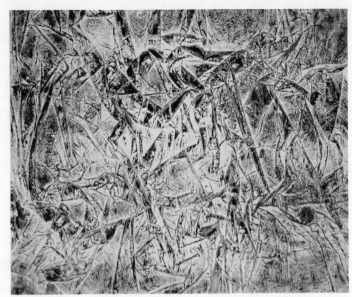

Young Woman with Butterfly in Throat by Henry Rasmusen. Thin pigment monotype. This work differs from a collagraph in that the discarded yarn and string used to create the figure were not glued to the Masonite, and much of the effect was achieved by loose brush work on the plate, using thin oil paints instead of stiff printer's ink, as is usual in a collagraph.

Insectville by Henry Rasmusen. Collagraph. This print was created by gluing cut and creased crepe paper onto the plate, then inking and printing.

Masks from paper bags. (From *Our Expanding Vision* by Fearing, Martin, and Beard, W. S. Benson Company, publishers.)

5.
Junk Sculpture in the Classroom

Children are natural junk artists. In their play they turn found objects to the need of the moment. A mud puddle makes a pie, a piece of newspaper, a discarded block of wood and a stick make a sail boat, a row of cardboard boxes becomes a railroad train. Young students require very little theoretical instruction; just a bit of enthusiasm from the instructor and some junk materials with which to work.

Usually, the higher the grade, the more introduction is needed to allay the student's fears concerning his ability, and also the correctness of using throwaway materials, plus perhaps a simple demonstration from the instructor regarding the visualizing and assembling of a sculpture. A field trip to some place where discards may be found can be an important part of the introduction to the subject, and for gathering materials.

Mirror by Donald Bowker.

(Three sculptures this row and one below left by students at San Francisco State Downtown Center, instructor Art Grant.)

War by Jonathan Wu.

God by Mark Gladden.

Help by Phyllis Bigelow.

Daniel Boone by Charity Martin. Children's class, San Francisco Museum of Art. (Photograph by Claire Isaacs.)

Totems from boxes. Elementary school class project, Art St. Peter, instructor.

Plant by Judith Chatham. Instructor, Diana Stigbert, Kingston High School, Kingston, New York. Made from discarded aluminum house-siding and natural berries.

Flowers by junior college student, J. Fred Woell, instructor.

Construction by junior college student, Art Education Department, University of Illinois, J. Fred Woell, instructor. (Photograph courtesy *School Arts* magazine.)

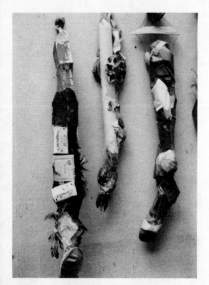

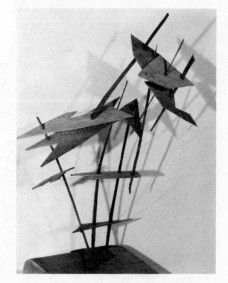

Stuffed nylon stockings. Students of children's classes, San Francisco Museum of Art. (Photograph by Claire Isaacs.)

Constructions (above and right) by high school students, Robert B. Kent, instructor. Plywood veneer.

San Francisco on a Foggy Day by Chris Menkin.

Right. Wash Room by E. J. Landuci.

(Both sculptures on this page by students at San Francisco State Downtown Center, instructor Art Grant.)

Sculptures by fourth grade students,
Florence Irving, instructor. They
are made from styrofoam coffee cups.
(Photograph by Jay Irving.)

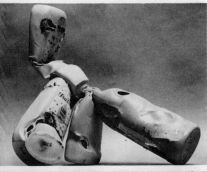

Construction by junior college
student, Art Education Department,
University of Illinois, J. Fred Woell,
instructor. (Photograph courtesy
School Arts magazine.)

Egg shell sculpture by Willie Mae
Belton, Concordia Teachers College,
Seward, Nebraska, Reinhold
Marxhausen, instructor.

Ship by Leroy Achterberg, Concordia
Teachers College, Reinhold
Marxhausen, instructor. Broken beer
bottle and light bulbs.

Beach Play

In beach play the participants enjoy the kind of happy and spontaneous exploration and creative fun usually associated only with children. They make the beach their kingdom and studio, drawing with fingers, feet, or sticks in the sand, whittling driftwood, making sand castings, constructing with beach wood, making mosaics from pebbles, seashells and pieces of beach glass, making assemblages with cans, bottles, and other discards, building sand sculptures, and carving bas-reliefs in sandstone cliffs.

Many of the works are temporary and impermanent, but the important thing is the satisfaction of creative play in the beach environment, which in itself is conducive to childlike, joyous expression.

Beach play is a good activity for all ages and groups—school, church, club, family, Scout, Campfire Girl, and so on.

A few items of equipment and materials may be taken along—a couple of hammers, a few nails, and some heavy cord for constructing sculptures with large boards and other driftwood, some white glue for bonding mosaic bits and pieces to wood backing, a few pounds of plaster of paris for sand casting, a large coffee can for mixing the plaster with sea water, a few half-gallon milk cartons for making plaster cubes to carve on, a pocket or utility knife for this, and a dinner knife for carving in sandstone cliff.

Beach play class, Art Grant, instructor. (Photograph by Edward B. Bigelow.)